in case of emergency press

We are proud to acknowledge the Traditional Owners of country throughout Australia and to recognise their continuing connection to land, waters, and culture.

We pay our respects to their Elders.

We support recognition, reconciliation, and reparation.

The Tercets

Jack Farrugia

in case of emergency press

http://www.icoe.com.au
Travancore, Victoria
Australia

Published by **in case of emergency press** 2023

Copyright © Jack O'Neill 2023

All rights reserved. Without limiting the rights under copyright reserved above, no part of this publication may be reproduced, stored in or introduced into a database and retrieval system or transmitted in any form or any means (electronic, mechanical, photocopying, recording or otherwise) without the prior written permission of both the owner of copyright and the above publishers.

ISBN 978-0-6456382-1-9

Photograph on cover and title page: **Clement Chapillon**.

Photograph of author: **Erin Comensoli**.

His are the feet
Which point the way onward.
There is no pilgrimage

Without asserting this
And there is no pilgrim
Without a pilgrimage.

This book is dedicated to Robin Ramzinski

Table of contents

Prologue I	1
Prologue II	3
I	4
II	5
III	8
IV	10
V	12
VI	13
VII	15
VIII	17
IX	19
X	21
XI	23
XII	26
XIII	28
XIV	29
XV	31
XVI	33
XVII	34
XVIII	36
XIX	39
XX	40
XXI	43
XXII	44
XXIII	45
XXIV	47
XXV	49
XXVI	50
Epilogue	52
Appendix I	54
Appendix II	55
Appendix III	56
Appendix IV	58
Appendix V	59
Appendix VI	61
Appendix VII	63
Appendix VIII	64
About the Author	67

The Tercets

Jack Farrugia

Prologue I

To find her
Black and gold
In the marbled shade

Of the terebinth,
Black and gold and painting
Horses coiled

In the cleanest abyss,
Here,
Black and gold

In the month of dew
And bedewed irises,
In the hydrated month

After the last frost,
To find her here
And black and gold,

To be so gently dislodged
From reality,
Is to press the bruise

Only so much as to draw
A certain pang of sweetness.
And who allots

This uncertain fruit
Of memory?
It is he

Who knows the fluid degree
Of pressure with which
To finger the bruise.

The wine-coloured mark
That is black and gold
Is black or gold

Depending on the status of
The impossible grape
That is the grape of hope,

But both black and gold
If the bruise is pressed
Only so much as to draw

The uncertain fruit,
The certain pang
Of sweetness.

PROLOGUE II

It is the cruellest path
That does not end, not even with
Death's homing gesture.

But his are the feet
Which point the way onward.
There is no pilgrimage

Without asserting this
And there is no pilgrim without
A pilgrimage.

I

Enter the desert nothingness.
And here he comes,
A knuckle of meat on stork-legs,

Battered by the gazes of nothingness,
Blistered by the climate of nothingness,
Governed by the nothing of nothingness.

Among the nothingness
The pilgrim kneels,
Kneads sand

Between
His fleshless fingers.
Myriad samples

Of textured nothingness.
Myriad
But not infinite.

II

Dog days are loosed
By horse-flies.
Cicadas drive the ceiling

Of their boiling pulse.
Life in the fiery drum endures.
Here, one must guard his eyes

From the glare and from
The flyblown noise.
The pilgrim must guard his eyes

And strive onward,
Seaward,
Across the shadeless undulations

Of sand and bone
And anaemic vegetations,
Here,

Where a gagged yearning simmers,
A yearning
For the kindness

That is mortal attrition.
Because this is
Mortal exhaustion. His is

A mortal exhaustion
To the score of seven centuries.
Seven trampled centuries of it.

How long
Must one go without
A mere slip of shade?

And what
Of her lovely mouth?
Will she come again, hiding,

As she often had, behind it?
You, who grappled Jacob
And submitted,

Let her come again
Hiding behind
Her poppy-red crooked lip.

O let it be
Then rip her free
From the poppy field of her hiding.

O let it be
For this life in the fiery drum,
This eternal becoming,

It is too hot.
It is too loud.
It is too much.

> *hush hush*
> *sh sh sh*
> *follow my voice*

III

Follow my voice, Weary Raven.
Follow my voice and hush
And hush.

So you ache to hear
A revelation?
But nothing at all

Shall ever be new
Beneath your belligerent sun.
Then what is it

You urge to be told?
Now pause
And hear this, Weary Raven.

There shall be
No fading yellow hour,
No final yellow whisper,

For such is the passage
Of your becoming.
But there was a terebinth

That shaded us
And there was a love
That loved us.

Do you remember, Weary Raven?
Do you remember the hum
Of citrus,

Those careful agitations
Of spring?
You begged

For us a seat
Within
The brazen bull

Before the deaf tribunal.
Do you remember that much?
Do you remember the trumpets

At your sentencing?
But yours are the feet
Which point the onward

And yet to what end?
And yet to no end?
For there is no home

Nor shade
Nor balm
Beneath your wailing sun.

IV

Bread will harden in drying mouths.
Sweat will sour in cracking palms.
Atrophy will multiply

Where the children are not,
But here they chant
With shade in sight. Shade

And a fount
And cupped hands
For the bronzing light.

A mass of black hair
And milk-teeth await
A moment, each by each,

To climb the greased pole
For a prize, a lamb
For some mother to dismember.

Let them be
While they are.
Let them be

Before they are not.
When they were
They will know.

They will long for shade
In the grove of skulls.
The pilgrim knows, blows onward,

Seaward, like a memory
Of the slightest shadow
Cast

From a splintered wing
Reclaimed only
In the ungettable shade.

But they are, they are,
Those who rave in the courtyard,
Those who plug up the archway.

They are, they chant.
They are until they are not.
And what is she?

And is she not?
And is she lost
To the grove of skulls?

V

Tending to his whip
Post-wrath,
Scrubbing at the blood-pulp,

He regards the broad harbour,
The harbour and the breadth
Of his debt.

A man must demonstrate
A peerless penitence
To prove that he possesses it.

Of this sentiment
The pilgrim is convinced.
But how much blood

Must be shed?
Yet another matter is blurred—
Is one still the master of

His instrument
Or is an insidious reversal
Of rank taking place?

VI

One can only reach so far.
Reaching backward,
One can barely scratch

The baptismal moment
From which
The second of his three lives

Was launched.
One can barely distinguish
The baptismal chrism,

A vial from the vein of Lethe,
And the baptismal garment,
Her fabrics

Tacked against his,
And the baptismal promise,
The most durable promise.

But one might sip
From the essence
Of the moment

Should one prick its crust
And this essence,
It is the crude black syrup

Of dreamless sleep. It is
To be totally submerged
In the reservoir of it,

To be there, adrift,
Where the black shapes
Of nightingales

Forfeit song to the silences
Of this black catatonia.
One can only reach so far,

Reaching backward
To the laying on of hands,
To his second genesis.

One can only reach so far,
And, at such an hour,
This far and no farther.

VII

The blond rock frothing
With black beards and cassocks
Is sunken

By the horizon.
Now the sun, risen,
Cresting, pulses loudest,

Chiming above briny murmurs.
And here, at sea, the flesh is ever
So firmly willing.

How it quakes to know
The scourging
And the shade of absolution.

And here it is, the whip, daring
Its very function.
How it burns to know

The passion and the pull
Of its direction,
Burning and burning to know

The surging and the spasm.
And here is the pilgrim,
Seething, beating

His breast with a knotted fist,
Granting his flesh to any Zeus
Who might annihilate it,

Finally, and seething yet,
Gnashing his teeth,
He hurls his whip

To those sunless oblivions
That do not stir,
Those tired carpets

At the clay-pits of the sea.
Silence.
Stasis.

Flagellation is the posturing
Of the sycophant.
It is a mode of masturbation

Or so she had said
Seven centuries ago
When painting her Judas,

A headless Judas,
Erecting bird-baths at the base
Of some Gemonian staircase.

VIII

See the hanged moon
Not spinning
Her suicidal comets,

Not grinning nor amused,
But trapping
The dizzy pilgrim.

See the flame in his hand
Levitate, lily-white.
A burnt wind

Transpires, trying the torch,
And the hanged moon stares
Her tundra-stare,

Exposing her concussion
To the pilgrim,
Chafing the naked cord

That binds him together.
Again
He turns

And there she is, the moon,
Illumined by the horror
Of confusion.

O the moon,
The hanged moon,
She now whets her slick jaw.

O the moon,
The blind seer,
Like a jackal she purrs—

A certain neighbour at
A certain hour should
Plead for his boat to sink.

IX

Through the hazes of cannabis
And kicked lime-dust,
Has one gone along this esplanade?

Has one gone among
These generations of salt merchants?
And what of those mackerel gatherers?

Vague faces all, suspiciously vague.
Here, a faceless figure
Adjusts his conical cap.

There, a cameleer
Pawns a three-legged calf.
And what of that dome yonder?

And what of this spire?
It is all too vague,
Too inherently vague. And what of

This trial in the nearest arena?
Hemmed in
By the multitudes

Like wounded game, three sisters
Stand accused of patricide.
It is much too vague an episode.

And farther on,
Beyond the city walls,
Jaundiced widows

Throw shadows
About the gleaning fields,
Shadows as lank as they are vague.

And yet farther on,
Where nothing grows,
One goes

Along the cart-ruts
Until they lose form
And there,

The pilgrim encounters himself
Waiting for himself
To suffer the desert once more.

X

Tonight
The moon is bloated
With a belly full of mockeries.

She rouses
From her mountain-side,
Flaunting

Her impressions
Of an upright man, a flagellant,
At once grovelling low

In thick mud
Like a beaten dog before a king,
A king that is an heir of Cain,

Cut from
The flagellant's rib
And his veiled sin,

That is the sin of lust,
Of lusting for
The polished mask of uprightness.

So arresting is the drama
And so finely acted
The pilgrim scarcely blinks.

Is the hanged moon unaware
Of another moon
Higher than herself?

Is she unaware
That above them both
Are higher moons yet?

It matters not
For she has cornered her prey
And drained the sleep

That had swum between them,
For she is now so near
As to shout in his face,

Now so near
As to hack apart the scabbing
Of his shame in its healing.

XI

Because these dog days sustain
The bloodless colours
Of baked rubble fences

And spans of wiped plains
And skies without lungs
And the many whitening colours

All sucked of vitality.
Because these dog days
Are bastardised

By belts of cicada-noise
And it is this merciless bawling,
This sound

Of bald heat throbbing,
Which scalds raw the shoulder,
Which halts the momentum

Of the one foot
And the other, the left foot
And the dogged foot,

The dogged foot
And the right foot,
The lame foot, the gasping

And the stagger,
Then the one foot and the other,
That which points the way onward.

Onward, onward,
But the plains are trackless.
Which is the foot that points

The way onward?
Does one drain the distance
Across these neutered lands?

Shall the gathered hand
Gouge out an abscessed tooth?
Do the hinges of the fingers

Still pinch at will?
Which is the foot
That points the way onward?

Where is the pot that keeps
The brown water?
Inspire one,

You who inspired Anthony
The Anchorite,
You who directed him

Into the desert.
Offer one the pork that he denied
And denied again. Tempt one

With a tear of opium
So that one may take his measure,
So that one may lean into the shade

Which is the mirage
Of maternal shade,
So that one

May blunt the screaming glare,
Because these dog days
Are utterly humourless.

XII

Pollen is afoot in the marbling light
Which warbles through the bones
Of the terebinth

So to glance
Her Roman nose and her black hair,
So to bless the vacant bench

For she stands as she had
After spurning death
Like a statuette in the dappled light,

In the half-lit shade,
Poised before her task
Like a granite monk.

And he dreams that she works
With urgency, milking an hour
Of clarity

In which she records
The interior of an artery
Reverberating,

And the sway of various vapours
Too transient to name
And royal crocuses

And the proletarian crocus
Gloating, trembling with pride
After the rain

And all that is swept to this side
Of mortality.
And he dreams

Of taking her painting wares,
Of making them clean,
Of sorting them

So as to be used again
And so he dreams of her
Working beneath the terebinth

And he dreams of watching her
In the act, in the morning,
In the silence,

And no taller
A privilege shall ever
Be uttered.

And so he dreams of Epictetus
Consoling Hadrian
In the catacombs

With a dish of figs, the philosopher
Pulling thorns of sorrow
From the emperor's heels.

One man howls in his private hell,
Another lounges in his dreams.
Which is he who owns his heart?

XIII

Selected barbs from the moon,
The hanged moon, on a night
Brutalised by an orange simoom.

Prometheus regretted nothing,
It is said, but I saw that he sobbed
And he sobbed like an orphan...

It should not escape thee
That many men and better men
Have known her lovely mouth...

You are a vile criminal, indeed,
But you are not Herod nor Caligula.
Those abominations were fathers...

Remember the length of her legs,
Run your eye along their length,
Run your hand along dry smoke...

XIV

The yawning day usurps the dawn.
The grape of hope is blistering.
Life in the fiery drum endures.

Buzzards cut rings about the sun.
Adders scream into studded skins.
Life in the fiery drum endures.

There is no mule to ride,
Not a disc of bread,
And there is no water.

Not any.
None.
There is no water

And too much clamour.
This heart,
It is a dog barking too readily

At what it cannot see
For the glare is too hot, too white.
Is one beholden to this heart?

Hear it thrashing now for shade
Like the muted desert shrub.
It is too much.

This must be what they speak of
When they speak of
Irrational numbers. This must be

What she painted
If she painted
Emaciation.

Life in the fiery drum endures
And it is too hot, it is too much.
And what is she?

And is she not?
And is she lost
To the grove of skulls?

XV

He is nothing of a stranger
When he arrives at this juncture.
Shrouded in an amber mist,

This is the place
Where all paths converge,
Where all paths are distilled

Until only two claw onward.
Two avenues beckon
And both arrive precisely

Where the other never must.
O indecision, how it quickens
Percussive blood.

But one shall choose the way
With the cool road underfoot.
One shall choose the way

Where a mortal he shall be
And so a mortal he shall be
Aiming for

The haunt of shade.
Grunting, wincing, hooking
His neck

Yet his are the feet
Which point the way onward
And one shall not loiter

Nor shall one doubt
But only exhale
For there is relief untold

Beyond these rusted breaths,
For in the deepest shade
The curtains of closure await.

> *hush hush*
> *come to me*
> *follow my voice*

XVI

Must she always transpire,
Always and forever,
At an hour such as this?

Yet again
Has the armour of resolve
Become like talc

And yet again will it crumble
To be scattered by the currents,
By the music

Of her Marian whisper,
Yet again and yet again
And always and forever.

He who vowed
Never to commit again,
Never to prostrate again

Before the familiar altar,
Is he who forsakes
The hallowed haunt of shade,

Is he who trips
Into the glare, is he who calls
And he who strains

And straining yet, striving forth,
Is he who calls
Her immaculate name.

XVII

Follow my voice,
Weary Raven,
And if only this once

Turn over your soul.
Allow its infamous side
To teach you

How
And to teach you when
To dampen the glare,

Then haul your body
Like another hauls
Copper from the quarry

And come to me
And come
And spit into your palm.

Sign in saliva
What you dare not mutter
And I shall hear it.

What is it, Weary Raven?
Open your hand.
Pursuing what is lost,

That mote of gold,
The rented leaf we lifted,
It's as if you are forever

Returning
To the one river,
Which both is and is not

The same river.
It has surely been plucked
Of its numbered riches.

We did this.
We made invalid amulets
And hung them

From the terebinth.
Do you remember this?
Do you remember

When
I cracked my head open
On the satin pillow?

That is how it is to live
In the temple
Of your exaltation.

Now come to me,
Follow my voice,
For all will be revealed.

Come, Weary Raven.
Let me show you where
I really live.

XVIII

Alone,
One and alone, the pilgrim
Squats in the chthonic dark.

One and alone,
Like an infant stranded
In the marshes of the fatal womb.

But what is this vault
Of fractured rock?
And by which name shall one call it?

This clotting air is more a broth
Of sediments and salts, of steam
Thinning

From the breath and shoulder.
But what is this centre without centre?
What is the bowel

Of the bowel of this dark?
And on whose counter is it forged?
And by which title is it called?

>   *this is where*
>   *I really live*
>   *come come and see*

And O
How swiftly the dark is drained
How the vault is drenched

In screeching light.
And there it is, the blazing image,
Splayed across the ceiling.

There,
Revolving, demanding
That nothing neglect its veracity.

There,
A slain gazelle with folded wings
And seven babes,

Hyenas each,
All shoving for place
By the barren breast.

> *this is where*
> *we really live*
> *this is harmony*

He speaks her name.
He speaks of the impossible grape.
He speaks of it again in a dead language

And the vault
Only shivers with chthonic babble.
And so his woe ascends itself,

Gathers its mass
Into itself, spumes
And erupts, and he slides into

A wretched laugh!
And how he laughs
And he laughs without recourse

For he knows
The name he has always known,
The name by which the dark is called.

And yet he laughs and he laughs
As the glare dissolves,
Laughing yet without relent,

Until the telling of truth
Is certainly told
And the chthonic dark

drips
drips
drips

XIX

The bruises of the gloaming
Are blackening.
A nightingale flinches

On a black branch
In the blackened bush.
And how

Shall one receive it,
This silhouette
That cannot be shared with her?

His time is not time
But an act of turning
And this implacable turning,

Black and lilac
At present,
It is all he has to regret it.

XX

Leaden clouds congregate
Over the desert.
Entire nations of them arrive

In drowsy caravans
So as to coalesce,
So as to establish a senate

From which to annunciate.
Truth
Has resurfaced

Thus doubt is abolished.
One shall mourn it urgently
Then move onward

For now truth prevails.
It is scrutinised,
Probed for faults in design,

But remains
Too horribly unblemished.
The truth remains glaring

Too whitely.
One must smother it.
There exists a black tapestry

Known best as denial
And it is woven with a twist
Of her black hair.

One shall construct for it
A cabinet
Of gratitude

That it shall be visited
At the dawning hour
Of each sand-bitten morning,

That its silks may duly serve
To gag the truth.
Doubt shall rise again

Where denial reigns
And only in doubt
Lives the greenest potential.

It is this potential alone
Which begets
The impossible grape

That is the grape of hope.
There is no pilgrimage
Without asserting this.

And lo,
The cloud-mass ruptures
From the navel

And the grey rains
Soothe
The scorched desert expanse.

These are not rains known
To surge across
The earth's crust

But rains that,
With delicate authority,
Rejuvenate the tissue

Of the trodden hyssop blossom.
These are rains that,
In the grasses of memory,

Liberate the vineyard
From the pits of melancholia.
And lo,

His shrunken husk
Dies among the rains
Before rising once a man

As when Lazarus had
While the orchards sang
The wealth of Mount Olivet.

XXI

All Orion's stars are nodding,
Steaming in their sockets.
Each to each

Bears witness there in ashes
And in sackcloth.
And they sing:

O and O, the beauty in
The business of
Defiance!

O and O,
And O and O,
O and O and O!

O and O, the glory in
The business of
Defiance!

O and O,
And O and O,
O and O and O!

XXII

His becoming in itself
Is never becoming
And his time is not time

But an eternal turning.
And though his trajectory
Is predetermined,

Though he is a prisoner
To this continuum,
To this life in the fiery drum,

This act of turning,
And though the mouth dries
And the bread hardens,

His are the feet
Which point the way onward.
There is no pilgrimage

Without asserting this
And there is no pilgrim
Without a pilgrimage.

XXIII

These are the final moments
Of his first life.
They are ignited by a sighting

In the fat of the garden. There,
Seated on an artichoke blossom,
A frog

Glossed in essence of
Eden-green,
Shaded loam.

Not ever has she witnessed
Such concentrated beauty
For she says so

With the lacquer of aged eyes
Now that of an untried innocent,
With eyes that come forth

From their hiding place
Behind her lovely mouth.
Yet watching her

Watch the frog,
He reaches to capture
That which remains unspoken—

What is this celibate combustion?
What is this soaring desire
To protect her?

And does she know for whom
It hungers?
Will she hail its sudden talons?

Will she feel them
Gliding
Through the slits in her ribs?

Has one dragged his feet
Like a flightless bird
For twenty-seven years?

XXIV

Now rise and hear this,
Weary Raven.
Seven yellowed centuries ago

When your sentence was enacted
And your shaven head was branded,
When you graduated

From iron bracelets
To the throes of eternal bondage,
It was decreed that my voice

Would not be raked
From your soul
But would remain to smoulder,

Only to steepen the heat
Of your torment.
And what might you say to that?

But remember the terebinth
That shaded us,
That and the love that loved us

For I have reminded you
Of such graces. Now go there,
Go there, enter that tent.

Go there to recline
And to convalesce.
Go there,

Go there
And ask yourself this—
Was it the terebinth

Or rather
The gift of its shade
That we sought to deify?

XXV

Enter the desert nothingness.
And here he comes,
A knuckle

Of juiceless meat, unwrinkled
By the bitter manna of nothingness,
Instructed

By the daily whisper
Of nothingness, unpardoned
By the daily nothing of nothingness.

As green as the tamarisk
That has sprung from salt,
As green

As the ghost of it,
Here he comes in the custody of
Due consequence alone.

> *hush hush*
> *sh sh sh*
> *hush*

XXVI

Come the rapid inhalation
Of a memory.
Here, in the lap of the terebinth,

She sources
A waft of divinity
By teasing a knot

From her black hair.
Her horses shall no longer idle
In the blankness of middle air.

No,
They are destined, her horses,
For some climate other

Where
Beards of lichen are strung
And the colour of moss

Adorns
The shade-coloured oaks,
Where their master's voice

Alone,
Is that of running water,
Of water running over

Water-oiled rock.
There, rid of heaven,
Washed in the hue of autumn,

Her horses shall be defined
By their uprightness
For this is her will,

For she is the painter
Of their becoming
And their becoming

Is now complete.
Her horses shall no longer idle
In the whiteness of heaven's glare.

Epilogue

Dry thunder tumbles
Over the acropolis of Alexandria,
Forcing upon the crane-masts

Some arthritic dance or another,
Awakening the last
Of Abbadon's locusts

From a mutilated shipping container.
The beast cannot elude death
Any longer.

Now perched atop Pompey's Pillar,
Obscured
By occasional fumes,

By the guttural airings
Of a world in ruins,
The beast surrenders its crown

To the fire beneath
For it cannot elude death
Any longer.

When the beast does fall
It will stay fallen.
The beast can no longer endure

But another must.
Alone, one and alone, the pilgrim
Squats in the fiery drum.

> *hush hush*
> *sh sh sh*
> *follow my voice*

APPENDIX I

Sans shaded couch.
Sans perfumed throat.
Sans flood of love.

Sans flute-music.
Sans flask of wine.
Sans humming love.

Sans gleaming axe
Of a love that chops.
Sans twin ribbons

Of incense-smoke
Dying in the breeze
Together.

APPENDIX II

It is engraved above a sundial:
Blessed be both
The unborn and the dead

Who host
A shaded place in time
For the common sun

Illuminates
One's smoking lot of woe.
Never a timepiece so punctual.

APPENDIX III

Their galleys flex
The muscle
Of a staunch mathematics.

Their figureheads
Are each a bust
Of a muscular Pythagoras.

They are astronomers
And cartographers
And far-sighted daughters

Cradled
Upon the balance
Of salivating waters.

Many are they and of fame
And four are their ships
And yet

They cannot divide
The pilgrim into four
Bloody parcels. And so

The scarlet flags are sent for,
Those badges of humiliation,
As the pilgrim

Cannot be broken. Long ago
He would have succumbed
If only

He were able to break.
So why then this sensation?
It is the agony

Of limbs being divorced,
By and by,
From the trunk.

APPENDIX IV

But the bats possess modes
Of silencing the heat.
See them unstitch from the heads

Of date-palms, one and the next,
Landing
With a dim thud

Like that of a dropped peach.
See them forming leaking heaps
Of death-scraps.

For now they own
The putrid death-musk.
It is theirs until

They are too far dead
And once too far
Is much too far for them.

With nostrils flared
The pilgrim passes
And life in the fiery drum endures.

APPENDIX V

That seminal happening,
How it now softens his blood
Like an opiate.

It is black and gold by memory
For she, then, was rendered black
And gold. Black

Of shawl, of hair and kohl,
Cast in black and gold
By shade of dusk and milk

Of torch.
In the wood above a marsh
Mushrooms are herded

By their patient shepherdess.
That is all.
Everything other is peripheral.

Even his misused god evaporates.
He cannot be stirred
By the leech taking root,

Nor by
The song of the nightingale,
One with all dissonance

Rinsed out of it.
That shade-laden awakening,
How it now softens his blood

Like an opiate.
And as he was then
So he is here, entombed in

The fizz-matter of paralysis
And everything other
Is peripheral.

APPENDIX VI

Tonight
The moon busies her wits
With the rebuking of

Orion's stars.
And so it begins.
She refuses their refusals.

She choreographs their sins.
She outnumbers them
Forty to one.

She decapitates their stoicism
With the dullest edge
Of her unhurried tongue.

Or so she tries.
They set their jaws.
Orion's stars

Brace
And parry the blows.
They cannot shy away

And they would not
Even if
They were able

For the tenet among them
Is such that,
In the amnesias of the future,

They may at last see the passing
Of all that has passed.
And so the hanged moon

Withdraws from her sport,
Stoops,
Squints,

Drags her tongue across
The wreck of her teeth
While other targets,

Chanceless targets,
Announce themselves—
Those for whom there is

No psychopomp
To bring death to the dead
Or to the dead of hope.

APPENDIX VII

Zero and infinity
Are both motherless entities.
Each is the surrogate mother

Of its counterpart.
Find them here
Plaguing the sum of his days.

Find them here,
Cheek against cheek,
Parading perfect symmetry.

APPENDIX VIII

And so his name was uttered,
Borne aloft
Like a poplar seed

Within her cotton breath.
And so his name was uttered
With a feline ferocity

Afoot
In the black of her eye. And so
His name was uttered, accented

By the pale winds
Of her ancestral lands.
And so his name was uttered

As they lounged in wild millet
If only for a moment
Of no consequence at all.

About the Author

Photograph of author: Erin Comensoli

Born in 1994, Jack Farrugia is a Maltese-Australian farmhand, amateur boxer, and poet.

The Tercets is Jack's first book.

www.ingramcontent.com/pod-product-compliance
Lightning Source LLC
Chambersburg PA
CBHW020329010526
44107CB00054B/2033